Richard Beales

In memory of Peter

Photos by Bruce Bennet Photography

Published by Willowisp Press, Inc.
401 E. Wilson Bridge Road, Worthington, Ohio 43085

Copyright ©1988 by Willowisp Press, Inc.

All rights reserved. No portion of this book may be reproduced, stored in a retrieval system, or transmitted, in any form or by any means, electronic, mechanical, photocopying, recording, or otherwise without prior written permission from the publisher.

Printed in the United States of America

10 9 8 7 6 5 4 3 2 1

ISBN 0-87406-325-6

TABLE OF CONTENTS

1. Wayne Gretzky (Edmonton Oilers) 5
2. Wendel Clark (Toronto Maple Leafs) 17
3. Ron Hextall (Philadelphia Flyers) 29
4. Pat LaFontaine (New York Islanders) 39
5. Ray Bourque (Boston Bruins) 51
6. Michel Goulet (Quebec Nordiques) 63
    Statistics 74

Wayne Gretzky set an NHL record in 1982 when he scored 92 goals.

WAYNE GRETZKY
Edmonton Oilers

The seventh game of the 1987 National Hockey League championship had reached the midway point. The Edmonton Oilers and the Philadelphia Flyers were locked in a 1-1 tie. The crowd tensed. Each team had won 3 games. The winner of this final contest would take home the league trophy, the Stanley Cup.

On the sidelines, Wayne Gretzky, the 26-year-old star center of Edmonton, could hardly wait to get back into the game. The young Oiler, wearing number 99 on his jersey, dug deep inside himself. He searched his tired body for that little bit of extra strength. More than 17,000 fans at Edmonton's Northlands Coliseum tensed. They waited to see if he could come through for them again this year. With just over 5 minutes left in the second period, Gretzky skated onto the ice with his linemates Jari Kurri and Esa Tikkanen. Could they score the winning goal?

Gretzky has what hockey experts call a "sixth sense." He always seems to know where the puck is going to be. Suddenly, like a bird of prey, Number 99 swooped on a loose

ABOUT WAYNE GRETZKY

Full Name Wayne Douglas Gretzky
Birthdate January 26, 1961
Hometown Brantford, Ontario
Family Single
Boyhood Hero Gordie Howe
Outside Interests Baseball; watching other pro sports; has dedicated his own charity, The Wayne Gretzky House, to the Canadian Association for the Mentally Handicapped; Christian Children's Fund; Canadian National Institute for the Blind; Canadian Juvenile Diabetes Association

Hockey-playing Relatives
Keith Gretzky (brother)—Rochester, AHL

---

puck. He swept a soft pass to Kurri. Kurri shot the desperately needed goal.

The Oilers ended up winning their third Stanley Cup in 4 years. And Gretzky had assisted on the winning goal.

"This is the biggest night of my life," he said after the victory, a broad smile on his face. "It would have been the biggest disappointment of my life if we would have lost."

It was no accident that Gretzky made the game's winning play. In the 1986–87 season, Wayne scored 183 points (goals plus assists) over the 80-game regular schedule. Even the great Kurri, who finished second in league scoring, was 75 points off Gretzky's pace. Gretzky is a gifted puck-shooter and an even better passer. When teams try to force him off the puck, he simply feeds it off to another Oiler. Often, his teammate is sent into the clear.

Despite his brilliant individual play, Gretzky is a team man. Personal records mean little to him. The only award that really matters is a team trophy—the Stanley Cup.

The Brantford Wizard

A native of Canada, Gretzky was born in 1961 in the small city of Brantford, Ontario. Most Canadian children enjoy skating. Some start before they begin school. Young Wayne took his first skate on the river which ran through his grandparents' farm when he was only 2 years old! He loved it. In fact, his parents had a hard time getting him back into the house after skating. When he was 4, his father built a small ice rink for him in the backyard. On it, a hockey legend began.

Wayne and his friends would skate or play hockey all day long. Sometimes, he would come inside with painfully sore feet (caused by the cold). But he never complained. He didn't want to be kept inside the house the next day.

At the age of 6, Wayne joined his first hockey team. His small size and young age didn't hurt his play. Few players could match his skill on ice. Those hours of practice on the backyard rink had really paid off. His passes were soft and accurate. His puckhandling was superb. His shot was tricky. When he was ten, he scored 382 goals in 82 games. That's more than 4½ goals every game! By the time Wayne was 11, people across Canada knew this boy had a bright future in hockey. Many could not remember such a skilled young player since Bobby Orr. (In the 1970s, Orr was one of the top players in the NHL.)

Hockey wasn't Wayne's only sport. He also starred at lacrosse and baseball. And Wayne isn't the only talented athlete in his family. His father, Walter, played hockey well enough to be a regular on a junior team. Before the 1980s, junior hockey was played by men aged 20 and under. Now, those who are 18 and under play in this league. Many

> **ABOUT WAYNE GRETZKY**
>
> **NHL Team** Edmonton Oilers
> **Number** 99
> **Height** 6'0"
> **Shoots** Left
> **Best Asset** Passing, stickhandling
> **Position** Center
> **Weight** 170 lbs.

junior hockey stars go on to become fine pro players on NHL teams. Wayne's younger brother, Keith, has also played several years of junior hockey in the Ontario league. Two other younger brothers, Glenn and Brent, also play hockey. People say Brent's talent will someday take him to the NHL, too.

Junior Star

At age 14, Wayne Gretzky and his parents made a daring decision. He would play junior-level hockey. Wayne was still small. Many fans thought junior players, some of whom were 19 and 20 years old, would break him in half with their crunching body checks. Wayne wasn't worried. He joined the Nationals, a Toronto junior "B" team, and proved he could survive. After scoring 2 goals in his first game as a junior, Wayne went on to score 60 points and win Rookie of the Year honors. The next year, he scored 72 points. Only 3 players in the entire league scored more that year.

Wayne's talent continued to draw attention. So did his hard work. At an age when many boys are delivering newspapers and watching TV at nights, Wayne was putting all his effort into playing hockey. Junior "A" teams from

Tight checking along the boards

the Ontario League were looking him over. They were getting ready for their annual draft of 16-year-olds. He was picked third overall by the Sault Ste. Marie Greyhounds.

The move from junior "B" to junior "A" is tough. But Wayne played brilliantly. He won Rookie of the Year and finished second in scoring with 182 points.

Wayne was prepared to play longer at the junior level. But the pros were watching him closely. At that time, players had to be 20 years old before NHL teams could draft them. But another pro league, the World Hockey Association, didn't have such a rule. The WHA was in trouble. It needed top players to keep its fans interested, but most of the stars were in the NHL. That meant going after "underage" juniors. Gretzky was the biggest name around. The WHA went after him, in hopes of proving that it, too, was a league of stars. So, in 1978, at the tender age of 17, Wayne Gretzky turned professional with the WHA's Indianapolis Racers.

Professional Powerhouse

Gretzky was an instant hit in the WHA. He impressed both opponents and teammates. One Racer defenseman, Kevin Morrison, was especially thrilled to have Gretzky on his team. "He's got more moves than a snake on a bed of hot coals," Morrison said of his new teammate.

Gretzky wasn't a Racer for long. The season was only 8 games old when the team ran into money problems. To help make ends meet, it sold Gretzky's contract to the Edmonton Oilers. The Oilers were a WHA team at the time. It wasn't until after that season that the two leagues merged. Gretzky was a big reason for the merger. He had signed a 21-year contract with the Oilers. The NHL knew that if it wanted this top player in its league, it would have to allow WHA teams in.

Gretzky's first professional year was a good one. In 80

> **WAYNE GRETZKY'S ACHIEVEMENTS**
>
> **Led League In**
> Goals: 1981–82, 1982–83, 1983–84, 1986–87
> Assists: 1981–82 through 1986–87
> Points: 1981–82 through 1986–87
> Assists in playoffs: 1982–83, 1983–84, 1984–85, 1986–87
> Points in playoffs: 1982–83, 1983–84, 1984–85, 1986–87
>
> **Important Trophies**
> Hart Trophy (1980, 1981, 1982, 1983, 1984, 1985, 1986, 1987)
> Lady Byng Trophy (1980)
> Art Ross Trophy (1981, 1982, 1983, 1984, 1985, 1986, 1987)
> Conn Smythe Trophy (1985)

games with the Racers and Oilers, he scored 110 points, was named Rookie of the Year, and won a spot on the second all-star team.

His greatest thrill came at the WHA all-star game. There, he played on a line with Gordie Howe. Many say Howe was the best player of all time. Howe had come out of retirement to play in the WHA. To Gretzky, it was an honor to line up on the same team as his boyhood idol.

"So Gretzky's been great in the WHA and the junior," many hockey fans said. "Just wait until he plays in the NHL, against the best in hockey. He won't seem nearly as good." But they were wrong. Boy, were they wrong! In his first NHL season, Gretzky scored 127 points—the league record was then 152—and tied for the league lead.

Gretzky kicks the puck ahead to his stick.

Gretzky was awarded the Hart Trophy as the league's Most Valuable Player. And the teenaged Oiler was the driving force behind the team's first-ever playoff finish.

The Record Breaker

In Gretzky's second and third years in the NHL, he set mighty individual records. What was more important to him, the Oilers got a lot tougher as a team. In the playoffs in 1980–81, the Oilers knocked off the always strong Montreal Canadiens in the opening round. Gretzky scored a hat trick—3 goals in 1 game—in the final game. But the team lost in the next round to the defending Stanley Cup champions, the New York Islanders.

Gretzky had had a great year. He set a new league record of 164 points. His 109 assists also broke a record.

Next year, in the 1981–82 season, the Oilers finished as the best team in the conference. If sports fans hadn't heard of Gretzky before, they caught an earful throughout that season. The slick center had always depended on his passing skills to get him most of his scoring points. Each year he played, he recorded far more assists than goals. Opponents were starting to get smart. They would check his wingers, so he would have no one to take his passes. But Gretzky outsmarted his opponents! He began to shoot more himself.

The results were astounding. By handling the puck more and using his excellent moves, Gretzky found himself with a lot of open ice. After just 34 games, he had 35 goals. Could he get 50 in 50? Only Montreal's legendary Maurice "Rocket" Richard and star Islander right winger Mike Bossy had ever done it before. Gretzky set himself to the task. He scored 3 goals against Minnesota, bringing his total to 38. He added 2 more against Calgary, and another against Vancouver. Then, he popped in 4 against Los Angeles. To get 50 goals in 50 games, he needed just 5

> ## WAYNE GRETZKY'S ACHIEVEMENTS
>
> ### Important Awards
>
> OHA Second All-Star Team (1978)
> OHA Rookie of the Year (1978)
> WHA Second All-Star Team (1979)
> WHA Rookie of the Year (1979)
> NHL Second All-Star Team (1980)
> NHL First All-Star Team (1981, 1982, 1983, 1984, 1985, 1986, 1987)
> Lester B. Pearson Award (1982, 1983, 1984, 1985, 1987)
> Emery Edge Award (1984, 1985, 1987)
> Chrysler-Dodge/NHL Performer of the Year (1985, 1986, 1987)
>
> ### NHL Records
>
> Assists in regular season (1981, 1982, 1983, 1985, 1986)
> Points in regular season (1981, 1982, 1986)
> Goals in regular season (1982)
> Assists in one playoff year (1983, 1985)
> Points in one playoff year (1983, 1985)

more in his next 14 games.

But Gretzky was never one to wait. The very next game, December 30th against Philadelphia in Edmonton, he scored 5 goals. The crowd at Northlands Coliseum roared as he scored the last one with less than a minute left in the game. 50 goals in 39 games! Gretzky, who had broken the record for assists the year before, was now the game's greatest goal scorer. Only one question remained: Could he score 100 goals over the full 80-game season?

Nobody in the history of the NHL had even come close. The all-time record, set by Boston's Phil Esposito in

1970–71, was 76 goals. But Gretzky tried. After 66 games, he had 82 goals. Only 18 more were needed, with 14 left in the season. Well . . . it almost, but not quite, happened. In addition to a new record of 212 points, Wayne Gretzky finished the year with 92 goals. It was the highest total ever.

Stanley Cup Years

Throughout the early years of his NHL career, Gretzky always had to listen to the same complaint: "Sure, you're breaking all kinds of records, but have you got what it takes to win the Stanley Cup?" In 1982–83, he and his Oiler teammates set out to silence the critics. Led by Number 99's 196-point season, the Oilers again finished first in the Campbell Conference. This time, there were no playoff upsets.

Edmonton knocked off team after team until they reached the Stanley Cup finals against the mighty Islanders. But the 3-time champion New Yorkers were too strong. The Islanders won the Cup in 4 straight games. Gretzky was held to just 4 assists. The Oilers could only say "Wait until next year."

Next year, they did follow up on that promise. Gretzky was as good as ever. During the regular season, he had topped 200 points for the second time. He carried his fine play into the playoffs. The young man from Brantford scored 2 goals and an assist in the final Stanley Cup game, helping the Oilers win their revenge. The team had come of age. It won the Cup from the Islanders in 5 games.

There was one important difference in the Oilers that year. Gretzky had been named team captain. Now the top scorer in the league had a new role. His teammates saw how hard their leader worked, and they, too, gave their best effort. His leadership paid off in 1984–85 with another Stanley Cup.

In the 1985-86 playoffs, the Oilers were upset by the Calgary Flames. Some fans began to have their doubts. Were the Oilers washed up? Had Gretzky lost his magic? It took a full year and the hard-fought 1987 final victory against Philadelphia, but the Oilers and their marvelous captain proved something important. They deserved to be mentioned with the greatest teams in hockey history.

WENDEL CLARK
Toronto Maple Leafs

Wendel Clark was frustrated. The Toronto Maple Leafs' 20-year-old left winger hadn't had a good scoring chance all game. It was a key game, too. The Maple Leafs and the Detroit Red Wings were in the seventh game of the NHL's Norris Division finals. Each team had won 3 games. The winner of this one would meet the Edmonton Oilers in the next series. And the winner of that series would play for the championship, the Stanley Cup.

Every time Clark tried to break free, he couldn't. He was being checked closely by Detroit's right winger, Joey Kocur. Clark and Kocur were both known around the league as fighters. Whenever the checking got too close, each man was known to drop his stick and gloves in order to fight.

Fighting is common in hockey. Many people don't like it. But it's there, and it's part of the game. Every team has 2 or 3 players whose specialty is fighting. Clark is one of the Leafs' toughest men. High penalty-minute totals are the sign of a fighter. In 2 years with Toronto, Clark had 498

> ## ABOUT WENDEL CLARK
>
> **Full Name** Wendel Lee Clark
> **Birthdate** October 25, 1966
> **Hometown** Kelvington, Saskatchewan
> **Family** Single
> **Boyhood Hero** Barry Melrose (cousin): first from Clark's hometown to make the NHL
> **Outside Interests** Fastball; working on family farm; Make-a-Wish Foundation (which grants last wishes for terminally-ill children)
> **Hockey-playing Relatives**
> Don Clark (brother)—Prince Albert–Saskatoon, WHL
> Kerry Clark (brother)—Saskatoon, WHL
> Les Clark (father)—Prince Albert, WHL
> Barry Melrose (cousin)—Detroit, NHL
> Joe Kocur (cousin)—Detroit, NHL

penalty minutes—and that's a lot.

But tonight, Clark wasn't fighting. People wondered why. Finally, the game ended. Detroit had won 3–0 and Toronto was out of the playoffs. Clark wouldn't say why he wouldn't fight.

After the game, a reporter asked Clark why he and Kocur didn't get into it.

"We won't fight," said the Maple Leafs player. The reporter kept pressing. Clark kept silent. Finally, Clark asked the reporter, "Do you want me to fight you?" The reporter wisely said no, he didn't. "Then be quiet about it," Clark said.

But there was a reason. Clark and Kocur were cousins.

Wendel Clark was snapped up as 1985 1st draft choice by the Leafs.

Both came from the same small town in Saskatchewan. Off the ice, they were also friends.

Wendel Clark is a rare young man. Even though he is a fighter, he has his principles. He won't fight dirty. He just comes at his opponent with his fists, fair and square. Clark is rare for another reason. He does far more than fight. He scores goals. On the ice, Wendel Clark can do it all.

The Kelvington Kid

Like most of the small towns in Canada, Kelvington, Saskatchewan was hockey-crazy. People would gather around their television sets on Saturday night to watch "Hockey Night in Canada." The Toronto Maple Leafs were usually playing. Little did anyone in Kelvington know that one of their young citizens would someday play for this great team!

Wendel Clark was born in Kelvington in October of 1966. The harvest was coming in on his parents' grain farm. From the day he was born, it seemed that Wendel was destined to be a hockey player. He was on skates at the age of 1½! By the time he was 3, he was playing organized hockey. He was younger than anyone else on the ice, but he wanted to play.

Kelvington people remember how dedicated he was. By the time Wendel was 7 or 8 years old, he lived for hockey. Other kids would get sick of the sport near the end of the long season. Not Wendel. Every morning he would get up at 6:00 and head outside. There, he would spend 2 or 3 hours shooting pucks into a hockey net. He'd still be at it when the bus came to pick him up for school.

Young Wendel used a special system to improve his shooting. First, he got a board the size of a net. Then, he cut holes out of the corners. He put the board in the net and started shooting. Every time he put the puck through one of the corners, he counted it as a goal.

ABOUT WENDEL CLARK

NHL Team Toronto Maple Leafs
Number 17
Height 5'11"   **Position** Left Wing
Shoots Left   **Weight** 190 lbs.
Best Asset Wrist shot

   Shooting for the corners is important. Imagine a goalie is in the net. The goalie and his stick will cover most of the middle. Any puck shot along the sides can be stopped by the goalie's arms. That leaves the corners. A shooter who can pick the corners will score more goals.
   When he was 12, Wendel played for 2 teams. One was in Kelvington. The other was in Yorkton, about 2 hours down the road. Whenever Wendel had a game in Yorkton, his parents would help him out—as long as he kept up his schoolwork. They picked him up after school. He would do his homework in the car. They would arrive in Yorkton, eat dinner, and take Wendel to his game. After the game, they'd get back in the car and Wendel would fall asleep on the way home. The next day, he'd be up at 6:00 again to shoot pucks into his net.

Talented Teen
   Wendel's pro hockey dreams came a giant step closer when he went to high school. At the age of 15, Wendel made the midget team at Notre Dame College in Wilcox, Saskatchewan. That was quite a feat. Notre Dame's teams have always been among the best in Canada. Here was Wendel, playing on the midget team with 16-year-olds.

Clark's all-out style often draws opponent penalties.

The coaches at Notre Dame were Barry McKenzie and Terry O'Malley. Both men had played on Canada's Olympic team. They knew talent. And they liked Wendel. "You kept waiting for the bubble to burst," said McKenzie. "It never did. From day one, he hit everything that moved and he's never stopped."

Wendel always played a physical game. There are 2 kinds of checking in hockey. One kind is stickchecking. A player will take the puck off his opponent by stealing it from his stick. The other kind is bodychecking. A good bodychecker throws his weight into the puck-carrier. When a body check is done right, the puck carrier is knocked to the ice. The checker winds up with the puck. Wendel has always been one of the best bodycheckers in hockey. He often leaves bruises on the players he hits.

After Wendel spent 2 years at Notre Dame, he was drafted by the Saskatoon Blades. The Blades are a junior team in the Western League. The Western League is one of 3 junior leagues in Canada that send top players to the NHL.

At Saskatoon, Wendel became a star. He played defense then, not left wing. Good defensemen keep opposing teams from scoring. Defensemen aren't expected to score goals or set them up. If they can, they're extra special.

Wendel could handle both defense and offense. His body checks knocked opponents almost out of their skates. His defensive work was good. And his offensive playing shone. At the end of his first year with the Blades, he had 23 goals and 45 assists for 68 points. Defensemen aren't *supposed* to score that high. But did Wendel mind?

His second year was even better. He scored 32 goals and had 55 assists. Now, pro scouts were starting to notice. Wendel's play was more than good. It was explosive. His coach, Marcel Comeau, put it best: "He's like a piece of dynamite in a tin can. He blows the lid right off."

Wendel's play earned him a spot on Canada's 1984 junior world championship team. This team traveled to Finland, a unique opportunity to match skills against top juniors from around the world. Canada went home with the gold medal, and Wendel was a big reason for the win. He played left wing for the first time and scored 2 goals in games against the United States and Sweden.

His biggest moment came not from a goal, but a body check. Canada's biggest rival in world hockey is the Soviet Union. Whether games are played by pros or juniors, Canadian and Russian competition is always exciting. Canada needed a win... badly. Early in the game, Wendel flattened Mikhail Tatarinov with a good, clean body check. Tatarinov had to be helped off the ice. The Soviets didn't stand a chance after that, and Canada won 5-0.

The pros loved it. Wendel was 18, and ready to be drafted into the NHL. He came into the draft as one of the favorites to be chosen first overall. Another was Craig Simpson, a center with Michigan State University. Who would be picked first? Simpson, an All-American? Or Clark, the Western League's top defenseman? Only the Toronto Maple Leafs (who held the first pick) knew for sure. And they weren't telling.

Toronto Tornado

On draft day, rumors swirled. Toronto general manager Gerry McNamara ended the gossip quickly—the Leafs chose Clark. Wendel was all smiles as he stepped up to the Leafs' table. They had a sweater waiting for him. On the front it had the team's traditional maple leaf emblem. The name "Clark" was sewn on the back. "We put the name on the sweater a week ago, if you want to know," chuckled the Leafs' owner, Harold Ballard.

When training camp opened, one big question arose: Would the Leafs play Clark at defense or on left wing?

WENDEL CLARK'S ACHIEVEMENTS

Led League In
Goals by a rookie: 1985–86 (34)

Important Awards
First over-all in 1985 Entry Draft (Toronto's 1st choice)
First All-Star Team, WHL (East Division), 1985
NHL All-Rookie Team (1986)

From the start, the coaches were thinking left wing. The Leafs had finished last in the league. They needed goal-scorers. They thought Clark could score more from left wing.

The move paid off. Clark was an instant sensation. In 20 games at left wing, he scored 10 goals. Toronto fans loved him and were already calling him a possible Rookie of the Year. But just as things were going great, a teammate's shot broke his foot. Wendel was out 14 games. He was badly missed, too.

Already, he had become a key player. He returned from his injury and continued his fine play. At midseason, he was named to play in the all-star game.

Other coaches and general managers liked him a lot for his fine, hustling play. At the end of the year, Clark had 34 goals and 11 assists for 45 points. Other rookies had more points. But few matched his overall fine play. The official Rookie of the Year award—the Calder Trophy—went to Calgary defenseman Gary Suter. But others preferred Clark. Both *The Sporting News* and *The Hockey News* called Clark their Rookie of the Year.

Clark fends off a stick check.

Toronto wasn't expected to go far in the playoffs for the 1985–86 season. But the Leafs beat Chicago easily. Then they took St. Louis to a full 7 games before losing the Norris Division final. Clark's hustle and hard work were big reasons. In 10 playoff games, he scored 5 big goals.

In 1986–87, his second year with the Leafs, Toronto came up with a plan for Wendel. The Leafs prized his scoring ability. They wanted to keep him on the ice. If Wendel was taking penalties, he wouldn't be there to put the puck in the net. Their plan called for him to stray less to deliver body checks. He would fight less.

As time went on, Wendel adjusted his game. He found he could play with more discipline and still find time for a body check or two. Clark was careful not to hurt the team by taking extra penalties for starting fights. His scoring totals remained high. He upped his goals to 37, and increased his assists to 23.

Clark even played a little defense at times. When the Leafs needed him, he was able to give the club a spark in that position. Still, he remained a left winger first and foremost.

The Leafs finished even better in 1986–87, Clark's second year. Again, they were strong in the playoffs. Clark sparked a first-round victory over St. Louis, then starred again in the series against Detroit.

At only 20 years of age, Wendel Clark was named an alternate captain of the Maple Leafs. He already meant that much to the team.

Ron Hextall can concentrate—even when the action gets furious! (Whoever said goaltending was easy?)

RON HEXTALL
Philadelphia Flyers

It was the start of a new season for the Philadelphia Flyers. On opening night, the Flyers hosted the mighty Edmonton Oilers. Both teams were hungry. They knew they were the 2 best clubs in hockey. And they both wanted the league championship trophy, the Stanley Cup.

Opening nights don't usually mean much. The NHL season is 80 games long. But that night meant a lot to one young man. Ron Hextall was playing goal for the Flyers. He had never played a game in the NHL before. The crowd didn't know it, but this was to be a fantastic debut for him!

Edmonton thought it would be an easy victory. After all, how can a raw rookie like Hextall be expected to stop the powerful Oilers? At first, they seemed to be right. The game was just 2 minutes old when the Oilers scored. Edmonton's Jari Kurri had deked Hextall easily. With 58 minutes still to play, the game looked like it might be a rout.

It didn't turn out that way. Hextall stopped shot after

> ## ABOUT RON HEXTALL
>
> **Full Name** Ronald Jeffrey Hextall
> **Birthdate** May 3, 1964
> **Hometown** Poplar Point, Manitoba
> **Family** Diane, wife
> Kristin, daughter (age 2)
> **Boyhood Heroes** Ed Giacomin
> Dan Bouchard
> **Outside Interests** Hunting; golf; watching Montreal Expos; Juvenile Diabetes Foundation
> **Hockey-playing Relatives**
> Bryan Hextall (grandfather)—New York Rangers, NHL
> Bryan Hextall, Jr. (father)—five NHL teams
> Dennis Hextall (uncle)—six NHL teams

shot. He stopped Edmonton superstar Wayne Gretzky on a breakaway. Gretzky came in all alone and shot, but Hextall kicked out his leg pad and stopped the puck. "Who is this guy?" the crowd buzzed.

The nervous rookie held Edmonton without a goal after Kurri had scored. After 2 periods, the score was still Oilers 1, Flyers 0. As the team started the third and final period, they knew the next goal would be a big one.

In the third period, Philadelphia tied the score. But Edmonton didn't give up. The big Oiler shooters kept coming at Hextall. He kept stopping them. A second goal gave Philadelphia the lead. Now, it was up to Hextall to hold the fort.

At home, Hextall's father and mother also were nervous. Tonight was the night their son made it to the NHL. But they couldn't get the game on television. They waited by

Hextall protects his net. (In the 1986-87 season, he led the NHL with a .902 save percentage.)

the phone and hoped he'd call with good news. The phone rang all right, but it wasn't Ron. It was a family friend who had been able to find the game on TV. He put the phone receiver up close to the TV so that Hextall's parents could hear it, too.

They listened as the broadcasters described the action. Their son's team was ahead 2–1 in the game! Could he hold on for the win? He did! The final buzzer sounded and Hextall leaped into the air. Gretzky and company had been shut out after that first shot. Hextall had stopped the Oilers!

Philadelphia coach Mike Keenan smiled. He had played a hunch and won. He had known deep inside that Hextall was ready.

The Flyer Tradition

The more Hextall played, the better he became. The Flyers won most of their games with Ron in goal. Hextall now was becoming part of a great Flyers tradition—good goaltending. In the Flyers' early years, they depended on a young goalie named Bernie Parent. The crowds loved Bernie for his spectacular saves. They chanted "Ber-nie! Ber-nie!" whenever he stopped a hard shot. Parent's career was followed by another great goalie, Pelle Lindbergh of Sweden. Unfortunately, Lindbergh died in a car crash early in the 1985–86 season. The replacement goalie did not spark fans as had Parent and Lindbergh. Who could fill the shoes expected of a great Flyer goalie?

Enter Ron Hextall. Until the 1986–87 season (when he began with the Flyers), Hextall had been playing with Philadelphia's "farm club"—a hockey team in Hershey, Pennsylvania, which was part of the American Hockey League. The AHL was only one step below the NHL.

After Lindbergh's tragic accident, the Flyers considered bringing Ron up to play. But they decided not to. The

ABOUT RON HEXTALL

NHL Team Philadelphia Flyers
Number 27
Height 6'2" Position Goal
Catches Left Weight 174 lbs.
Best Asset Challenges shooters

young goalie needed more time to learn. The decision was tough, but right. Hextall had been playing pro for less than 2 years.

When the new 1986–87 season started, Hextall "had only an outside chance of staying here," said coach Keenan. "He had to impress a lot of people." And he did. By the time the season was only a month old, the Flyers decided to make Hextall their number one goaltender.

An NHL Family

Ron Hextall seemed destined from the beginning to play in the NHL. It's a tradition in his family. His grandfather, Bryan Hextall, Sr., had been one of the best New York Rangers ever. For 10 years this all-star was a favorite of New York fans. In 1940, he scored a goal against Toronto in overtime to give the Rangers the Stanley Cup. When Bryan Sr. retired, he was elected to the Hockey Hall of Fame.

His young sons, Bryan Jr. and Dennis, also made it to the NHL. Bryan Jr. broke into the league in 1962–63 with his father's old team, the Rangers. He played 8 years with 4 NHL teams. In 1964, his son Ron was born.

Dennis, Ron's uncle, played 12 years in the NHL with 6 different teams. One year, 1972–73, he scored 30 goals.

Both sons of Bryan Hextall, Sr., were tough players. Neither ever surpassed the reputation of their father, but their teammates knew they could count on a Hextall to help them out of tough scrapes.

Hockey is a rough game. Fighting often breaks out. In the days when Parent was the Flyer goalie, Philadelphia was probably the roughest team in hockey. Some teams were afraid the Flyers would bully them, but the Hextalls were always ready.

Bryan Jr. and Dennis used to hate the Flyers. But now that Ron plays with that club, they are big fans of the team. For the Hextalls, family pride always comes first.

Ron got his start in hockey early. He and his brother Rod used to hang around their father's practices. They'd skate when the team was finished. Sometimes the players would stay and work with them. Jim Rutherford, the Detroit goalie, knew Ron wanted to be a goalie, too. He helped young Ron out. He even gave the boy one of his old masks to wear.

When Ron played minor hockey, his parents wouldn't let him play goal. His dad knew how easily a goalie could get hurt. But Ron loved the position. His mother remembers him as a 3-year-old, standing in goal for street hockey games. By the time he was 8, he was in net for good.

Once Ron was in goal, his father never tried to talk him out of it. He saw how Ron would sit behind the goalies at NHL practices, looking for tips. When Ron was 10, his father played for Atlanta. The Atlanta goalie, Dan Bouchard, showed Ron how to move in net.

The training helped. Because of what he had learned from NHL players, Ron made the Brandon junior team at age 17. Then, in 1982, the young goalie got his break. Ron was drafted by Philadelphia. "I think the name Hextall had something to do with the Flyers drafting Ron," said his uncle Dennis.

Hextall jumps to corral a high drive.

> **RON HEXTALL'S ACHIEVEMENTS**
>
> **Led League In**
>
> Save percentage: 1986–87 (.902)
> Minutes played: 1986–87 (3,799)
> Playoff minutes played: 1986–87 (1,540)
> Wins: 1986–87 (37)
> Playoff wins: 1986–87 (15)
>
> **Important Trophies**
>
> Vezina Trophy (1987)
> Conn Smyth Trophy (1987)
>
> **Important Awards**
>
> AHL First All-Star Team (1986)
> AHL Rookie of the Year (1986)
> NHL First All-Star Team (1987)
> NHL All-Rookie Team (1987)

Flyer Freshman

The Flyers stayed hot through Ron's rookie season. This Hextall kid must be good, people around the NHL thought. As the season wore on, he proved that he was. By the all-star break in February, the rookie led the league in several categories—including most wins and most saves. The league knew he was good. The NHL honored Hextall by picking him to play against the Soviet Union's national team at the all-star break.

Ron Hextall is a different kind of goalie. He's not only great at stopping goals, he is good with his stick. Maybe it's because his father and uncle were both forwards. Ron actually scored 6 assists over the year. Assists are passes which lead to a goal.

Some people think Hextall will someday even score a goal. In the 70-year history of the NHL, only one goalie has ever scored. (Billy Smith of the New York Islanders was awarded a goal in 1979. Smith was the last to touch a puck that an opposing player accidentally shot into his own net.)

Hextall wants to score a *real* goal. "He can do it," said teammate Dave Poulin. "In practice, Ron will hit the corners of the net from center ice."

At the end of the 1986-87 season, Hextall was voted first-team all-star in goal. But Hextall only wanted to win one thing: the Stanley Cup.

Stanley Cup Hero

With Hextall in net, the Flyers won 3 hard-fought playoff series during the 1986-87 season. Then they met their old rivals, the Edmonton Oilers, in the Stanley Cup finals. Edmonton won 3 of the first 4 games. The Oilers needed to win only 1 more. But Hextall stood strong. In Game 5, the Oilers built a 2-0 lead. Then Ron shut the door. The Flyers won, 4-3. In Game 6, it was the same story. Edmonton went up 2-0. Hextall buckled down. The Flyers won again, 3-2.

Philadelphia rallied around its goaltender. Could they come back to win 3 straight games and the Cup? In the finals, Hextall played as well as he had all through the playoffs. But Edmonton was just too strong. The Flyers lost, 3-1. Flyers captain Poulin praised Ron's effort. "Ron Hextall kept us in it," Poulin said. "He kept us alive, but we couldn't get the goals we needed."

The goalie managed a smile after the game, though. He was awarded the Conn Smythe Trophy as playoff MVP—just like Bernie Parent, who was now his goaltending coach. Hextall thanked the presenters, but said he'd trade the award for a Stanley Cup any day.

But the honors weren't finished. At the NHL awards

banquet in the spring of 1987, Hextall won The Vezina Trophy. Parent had won it twice. Lindbergh had won it once. Now, Hextall joined those 2 among the great Flyer goalies.

Still, Hextall wasn't quite satisfied. "I'm striving to be the best goalie ever," he said at the banquet. People who had seen him play realized that, with Ron Hextall, that was very possible.

PAT LaFONTAINE
New York Islanders

The New York Islanders were up against the odds that night in 1987. It was the sixth game of the NHL's Patrick Division semi-finals. Their opponents, the Washington Capitals, needed just 1 more victory to win the series. The Islanders needed 2. The plucky New York team had already battled back once to take Game 5. Could they do it twice more?

The Capitals were a powerful team. By midway in the second period, they had grabbed the lead, 3-2. They were ready to wrap up the series, 4 wins to 2. But they were overlooking Pat LaFontaine, the 22-year-old star center for the Islanders.

LaFontaine is only 5-foot-9 and 170 pounds. That's small for a hockey player. But he has a heart for the stiff challenge of hockey competition. LaFontaine just skated all the harder when the Islanders fell behind. He was determined to win the game for them. Just 2 minutes after the Capitals had gone ahead, Pat scored the tying goal. Three minutes after that, he passed to teammate Mikko

> **ABOUT PAT LaFONTAINE**
>
> **Full Name** Patrick Michael LaFontaine
> **Birthdate** February 22, 1965
> **Hometown** Pontiac, Michigan
> **Family** Marybeth, wife
> No children, but two dogs—Fred and Barney
> **Boyhood Hero** Guy Lafleur
> **Outside Interests** Coaching amateur athletes;
> Arthritis Foundation; Leukemia
> Society of America
>
> **Hockey-playing Relatives**
> John LaFontaine (brother)—Toronto, OHL

Makela. Makela scored!

The Islanders were ahead 4-3. But LaFontaine wasn't through. Two minutes later, he scored his second goal of the game. The Islanders were ahead 5-3! And LaFontaine had been the reason. He had scored 3 points in just 7 minutes. The Islanders held on to win, 5-4.

Now the series was tied at 3 wins each. The final game was set to be played in Washington. Winning in New York was tough enough for the Islanders. Could they reach down and beat them once again—this time in the Capital Center? LaFontaine and his teammates thought they could.

In the third period in Washington, the Islanders got a goal from their veteran star, Bryan Trottier. That tied the score at 2-2. Somebody would have to score again soon, or the game would go into overtime. But both teams held their ground. The 3 periods of regulation time ended with the score knotted at 2-2.

They skated out to face the first overtime period, 20 grueling minutes of tense hockey-playing. It was a "sudden

Number 16 redirects the puck while being crosschecked from behind.

death" situation. The first goal scored would clinch the win. The loser wouldn't have another chance. Because it was the final game, the whole series had come down to just one goal. But the overtime came and went without a goal scored. That wasn't too unusual. Often, teams will play a full period without a goal. But then something unusual did happen: the second overtime period also finished scoreless. Both goalies had played brilliantly, stopping shot after shot. Then the teams battled out a third overtime period. It, too, was goalless.

Now the players were exhausted. They had played 2 full games of hockey. The team trainers tried to help. They gave the skaters potassium pills and high-energy liquids. (Potassium is a mineral the body loses when it's overworked.) The Islanders needed a hero quickly, before someone collapsed on the ice.

The fourth overtime period was half over when LaFontaine answered the call. Pushing his legs for a little extra energy, he drove to collect the rebound of a shot from teammate Gord Dineen. LaFontaine raised his stick and slapped the puck as hard as he could. It hit the inside of the goalpost and spun into the net. The Islanders mobbed their hero, hugging him in thanks for his glorious goal. They had just won the longest NHL game in 44 years!

Young American

Pat LaFontaine learned to skate at age 3. By the time he was 7, he was playing organized hockey. That wouldn't be so unusual if he were a Canadian, like many NHL players. But Pat was born in St. Louis, Missouri. Like most American cities, St. Louis did not go crazy over hockey. It is not considered a big sport like football, baseball, and basketball.

Like most American boys, young Pat's friends played other sports, not hockey. But not Pat. He loved hockey

ABOUT PAT LaFONTAINE
NHL Team New York Islanders
Number 16
Height 5'9" **Position** Center
Shoots Right **Weight** 170 lbs.
Best Asset Quick-release shot

from the beginning. His father, John, was a Canadian. He told his two sons, Pat and John Jr., all about the game. He told them about the NHL and the great stars who have played there. So even though they lived in Missouri, the two boys dreamed about being pro hockey players. When the family moved to Pontiac, Michigan (a suburb of Detroit which is close to Canada), they were delighted. There are only a few states in the U.S. where hockey is a favorite pastime. Michigan is one of these hockey hotbeds.

Now Pat and John Jr. lived in a state that loved hockey. What could be better? The two boys were playing against good competition, near the arena where hockey superstar Gordie Howe used to play for the Detroit Red Wings.

John Jr. was older than Pat by a year. Even though Pat was younger, he was allowed to play with boys John's age. Coaches didn't care that he was small. He was talented and determined, and that made all the difference.

Detroit has an excellent hockey system for young students of the sport. Players from that city often develop as quickly as players from Canada. When Pat was "midget" age—16 years old—he played for Detroit's best minor hockey team. He was the star. In 79 games, he scored 175 goals and assisted on 149 others. That figures out to more than 4 scoring points every game he played!

Mixing it up along the boards

Scouts from Canada's 3 major junior leagues were watching. Pat was drafted by the Verdun Juniors. Verdun is a suburb of Montreal. Pat's boyhood hero, Guy Lafleur, was finishing a brilliant career with the Montreal Canadiens. Now, Pat was going to play in the same city. Everywhere he went, there were reminders of Lafleur.

Junior Record-Breaker

Fans in Montreal come from a long tradition of hockey-watching. They know good players and good teams. When LaFontaine brought his great midget record to Verdun, they weren't impressed. "Four points a game in midget?" they said. "Big deal. Let's see how he plays in a tough junior league."

LaFontaine proved to the doubters that American hockey players can be as good on ice as Canadians. In fact, he showed them he was better that year than any Canadian-born player in the Quebec League.

Yes, 1982–83 was LaFontaine's year. He started quickly. After his first 11 games, he had 11 goals and 19 assists. The fans' faith in him increased. He was on course for a 200-point season. Verdun fans loved him. With LaFontaine showing his magic, fans flocked to see the Juniors.

LaFontaine. Lafleur. Montreal now had *two* hockey heroes. By the time the league stopped play for its Christmas break, the young American center was big news. He had scored at least 1 point a game for 40 games in a row. That tied Lafleur's record, set back in 1970–71. The fans were anxious. Could the young American pass the great Lafleur? In his first game back, LaFontaine answered the question. He didn't score 1 point. He scored *4*. He popped in 3 goals and scored an assist as Verdun beat Granby 10–7. His name made the same record book as his hero.

Lafleur himself was happy to see LaFontaine play so

well. When the young junior broke the old pro's record, guess who was right there to congratulate him? Guy Lafleur!

The streak ended after 43 games, but LaFontaine had made his mark. In his first year of junior hockey, Pat LaFontaine had become one of the greatest players ever. At the end of the regular season, he had 104 goals and 130 assists for 234 points. He set the record for most goals, assists, and points by a rookie. He led the league in all 3 categories! Most importantly, he set a new league mark with 17 game-winning goals.

It's hard to top a record-breaking season. But LaFontaine managed. He played even better in the playoffs and led Verdun to the championship of the league. Overall, he scored 11 goals and 24 assists in the playoffs. He was named winner of the MVP award. The MVP trophy was named after—you guessed it—Guy Lafleur.

Now, it was time for LaFontaine and Lafleur to play in the same league. By the time LaFontaine was 18, the NHL had started drafting top 18-year-old juniors. Because he was rated so highly, the world champion New York Islanders took him in the first round.

The Islanders' general manager, Bill Torrey, was pleased. He said LaFontaine was the best player available in the draft. The Islanders had won 4 Stanley Cup championships in a row. Now, with LaFontaine on board, they could be on their way to 5.

Olympic Team Star

There was only one question: Would LaFontaine start the season in New York? The U.S. Olympic team also wanted him badly. LaFontaine was torn.

Finally, he decided to play in the Olympics. He knew that when the games were over in March, the Islanders would still want him. He could join the Islanders before

> **PAT LaFONTAINE'S ACHIEVEMENTS**
>
> **Led League In**
> Goals by an American-born player 1986–87 (38)
>
> **Important Awards**
> Third over-all choice in 1983 Entry Draft (NY Islanders' 1st choice)
> QMJHL First All-Star Team (1983)
> QMJHL Most Valuable Player (1983)
> QMJHL Most Valuable Player in Playoffs (1983)
> Canadian Major Junior Player of the Year (1983)
> 1984 United States Olympic Team

the NHL's regular season was over. And of course, he could still play in the playoffs.

The Islanders wished him well. Four years earlier, they had a similar case on their hands. They held the rights to defenseman Ken Morrow. Morrow decided to play in the Olympics, and he was glad he did. In the 1980 Olympics, the U.S. had a great hockey team. The Americans weren't supposed to win, but they went unbeaten. In an incredible final game, they beat the Russians for the gold medal.

The memory was sweet for many Americans. LaFontaine was 15 when it happened. He remembered the pride he had felt. He knew, if he was lucky, he could have the same double thrill as Morrow. He had a chance to win a gold medal *and* a Stanley Cup in the same year.

In pre-Olympic games, LaFontaine was an immediate hit. He was the leading scorer on the team. Torrey was impressed. "He's very intelligent," the Islanders' general manager said after watching the Olympic team work out.

"He always seems to be in command of the puck and has great puck instincts."

Unfortunately, not even LaFontaine could help the Olympians in 1984. The team finished seventh in the tournament. Pat also had fallen sick with the flu. He still played, and gave 100%. But his game wasn't as strong as usual.

NHL Newcomer

LaFontaine joined the Islanders for the last month of the 1983-84 season. He was well again and ready to play. Islander fans were anxious to see the young Olympian in action. In just his second game, Pat scored 3 goals and 2 assists as New York bombed Toronto 11-6. No Islander rookie had done that since Trottier, in 1975.

The rest of the season LaFontaine looked like the great scorer he was in Verdun. In 15 NHL games he scored 13 goals and 6 assists. Then came the playoffs. LaFontaine played well throughout them. He scored 3 goals and 6 assists in 16 games. But the Islanders were not to win the championship again this year. The young Edmonton Oilers (led by the great Wayne Gretzky) dethroned the champs.

LaFontaine came to training camp ready for a big year in 1984-85. It didn't happen, though. For the first time, he had problems. They began before camp when he sprained his knee in practice. Then, a month into the season, he was hit by mononucleosis. Mononucleosis is a viris that saps a person's strength. Pat managed to finish the year strongly, though, despite the odds against him. He was not quite strong enough, however, to be named Rookie of the Year.

The next season was just as frustrating. In midseason, LaFontaine suffered another injury. It took him 5 weeks to recover from a separated shoulder. LaFontaine found the NHL a tough place to play. He knew that he, too, would have to toughen up.

Pat lets fly a fiery puck shot. This guy likes to score!

In 1985–86, LaFontaine made a change. He stayed just as much of a scoring threat. But he started hitting people. He paid more attention to defense. And he hustled more. The results were good. He was one of the Islanders' best all-around players. By the end of the year, he had 38 goals and 32 assists for 70 points—his best season ever. And more importantly, Pat hadn't missed any games. Illness and injury were things of the past.

Watch out for Pat LaFontaine. He's about to take his place as the game's first American superstar.

RAY BOURQUE
Boston Bruins

Ray Bourque was nervous the night of June 10, 1987. It was almost worse than pregame jitters. The Boston Bruin defenseman was up for an award. *The* award, actually—the Norris Trophy. Every year, the National Hockey League honors its best players at a special ceremony. Among the awards is the Norris Trophy, given to the league's best defenseman. Many people had told Bourque he should win it.

But Bourque wasn't convinced. He had heard it before. During his 8 years in the NHL, he was always among the best defensemen. He had been named first-team or second-team all-star 7 times. The eighth all-star selection was almost certain. But he had never won the Norris Trophy. "A lot of people say I'm the best," he said, "but until my name's on the trophy, *I* can't say I'm the best."

That night, Bourque joined the large crowd at the Metro Convention Center in Toronto. Many of the top stars in the league were there: Gretzky, the league's MVP and scoring champ; Hextall, Philadelphia's great rookie goalie; Luc Robitaille, the young Los Angeles star. It was an honor to

> **ABOUT RAY BOURQUE**
>
> **Full Name** Raymond Jean Bourque
> **Birthdate** December 28, 1960
> **Hometown** Montreal, Quebec
> **Family** Chris, wife
>   Melissa, daughter (age 4)
>   Christopher, son (age 2)
> **Boyhood Heroes** Guy Lapointe
>   Serge Savard
>   Larry Robinson
> **Outside Interests** Golf; watching baseball
> **Hockey-playing Relatives**
>   Richard Bourque (brother)—Sherbrooke, QMJHL

stand among these hockey greats.

A major challenger to Bourque was Philadelphia's Mark Howe. Howe was the son of another great hockey player, Detroit's Gordie Howe. Mark was a fine player in his own right. He, too, could be a Norris winner.

The presentation was at hand. Bourque felt his stomach muscles tighten. Would his name be called? It was! He stepped up to the podium to accept it, a very proud young man. Now, he could say he was the best defenseman in the NHL. Out of 54 people who had voted on the trophy, 52 gave their first-place vote to Bourque. The 27-year-old star was finally recognized as the best at his job.

Before the night was out, Bourque enjoyed another victory. He had been named to the first all-star team for the fifth time. What a night!

Montreal Youth

It is funny that Ray wound up with the Boston Bruins. As a boy, he loved the Montreal Canadiens. He didn't

Bourque controls the puck. Like Bobby Orr before him, Bourque can shoot as well as defend.

know they'd be his greatest rivals when he grew up. Ray used to root for 3 Montreal players in particular. He liked Serge Savard, Larry Robinson, and Guy Lapointe. All were defensemen. All were NHL all-stars. And most importantly, all were winners. They played major roles in the Montreal teams that won 4 Stanley Cups in the 1970s. Montreal had a high-powered offense then, led by scoring champ Guy Lafleur. But young Ray's attention always turned to the defense.

Ray was born in Montreal in 1960. He remembers always being a hockey fan. When he was little, he would watch the Canadiens on TV. But he couldn't see the end of the games. He had to go to bed early and wait until morning to find out who had won!

Ray didn't start skating until he was 5 or 6 years old. But once he laced his skates, hockey wasn't far away. As he grew older, he had to go to bed even earlier. Practice was before school, and that meant getting up at 5:00 A.M. Ray's parents were very helpful. His father, Ray Sr., always drove him to practice. It didn't matter what time it was. If Ray Jr. wanted to play hockey, his dad would help out.

Ray wasn't always a big scorer. He mostly practiced his defense. His job was to try and break up scoring plays, not start them. He tried to imitate the Canadiens' big 3 defensemen. As Ray got older, his play improved. He found he could help his teams by rushing the puck. He had started becoming a two-way defenseman. He still played well in his own zone, but he had also become a scorer.

Blossoming Junior

When Bourque was just 16, he started major junior hockey. He played for the Sorel Black Hawks of the Quebec League. As a rookie, he scored 12 goals and 36 assists for 48 points. Those are good totals, but nowhere near the numbers he would later produce.

> **ABOUT RAY BOURQUE**
>
> **NHL Team** Boston Bruins
> **Number** 7
> **Height** 5′11″ **Position** Defense
> **Shoots** Left **Weight** 205 lbs.
> **Best Asset** Puck control

In his second year of junior, he played closer to home. The Black Hawks had moved to Verdun, a suburb of Montreal. Bourque enjoyed playing for the hometown crowds. And they loved him. Quickly, he was becoming one of the league's most dazzling players. Bourque was everywhere. He moved opponents off the puck. Then he picked it up and skated down the ice. Two, sometimes 3, opponents would be left sprawling as he shifted into high gear. At the other end, he'd pass off to a teammate who was in scoring position. Sometimes, he'd shoot the puck himself and score.

He ended the year as the second highest-scoring defenseman in the league. And he was a team leader. When the next season, 1978–79, started, Bourque was named captain.

Few players in hockey can "control the game." Bourque could, even as a junior. When he wanted the game to speed up, he'd skate at a furious pace. It was up to the others to catch up with him. When he wanted the game to slow down, he'd depend on his stickhandling. He'd kill time by "ragging" the puck, daring his opponents to catch him.

And Bourque is an iron man. Hockey games are 60 minutes long. Bourque usually played as many as 45 or 50 minutes. That's an incredible amount of time—most

Bourque rides New York Islanders' Bryan Trottier out of the play.

players would get exhausted.

Bourque was 18 when he had his tremendous junior year. That year, the NHL changed its rules. They could now pick junior players to play pro. Now, the league could draft 19-year-olds. That made Bourque available. The Boston Bruins had eighth pick. They took the young Verdun defenseman, knowing he would be ready.

Rookie Rearguard

Ray Bourque had finally made it to the NHL. But being young, he would sometimes get lonely on road trips. He would call home to Montreal just to talk with his family. One month he spent $185 on telephone calls! The first time he was in Los Angeles, he phoned home to tell his father about all the palm trees. It was the first time he'd ever seen them.

Most players break into the NHL slowly. If they were big scorers as juniors, they are often only so-so in their first NHL year. Not Bourque. He didn't play like a rookie. He played like a veteran of many years. Teammates and opponents marveled at his skill. "He's the finest rookie defenseman I've ever seen come into the league," said long-time Bruin star Brad Park.

Park, the veteran, was Bourque's defense partner. Together they would line up as "point men" for the power play. "Power play" is a hockey term for teams that play with 6 men on the ice while their opponents only have 5. (The opponents have lost the use of a man because of a penalty.) Point men are important to a good power play. They work at the far end of the zone, closest to the center, to control the puck in the enemy zone. A good point man must pass well, shoot hard, and control the puck. Bourque was gifted in all 3 areas.

In his rookie year, Bourque scored 17 goals and 48 assists for 65 points. No rookie defenseman on the Bruins

> **RAY BOURQUE'S ACHIEVEMENTS**
>
> **Led League In**
> Goals by a defenseman: 1980–81, 1986–87 (23)
> Assists by a defenseman: 1986–87 (72)
> Points by a defenseman: 1986–87 (95)
>
> **Important Trophies**
> Calder Memorial Trophy (1980)
> James Norris Memorial Trophy (1987)
>
> **Important Awards**
> Eighth over-all choice in 1979 Entry Draft (Boston's 1st choice)
> NHL First All-Star Team (1980, 1982, 1984, 1985, 1987)
> NHL Second All-Star Team (1981, 1983, 1986)

had ever scored more. Part of the reason was Park. The older defenseman was like a coach on the ice. Park has always known a lot about the fine points of hockey. Later, after he retired, he actually became a coach. For Bourque, he was a personal tutor.

Under Park's guidance, Bourque blossomed. He was named a first-team all-star in his very first year. He also won the Calder Trophy as Rookie of the Year. Many top stars started their careers by winning the Calder. All-time great goalies Terry Sawchuk and Glenn Hall won it. So did the New York Islanders' top scorer, Mike Bossy. And so did Bobby Orr.

In the Footsteps of Bobby Orr

Ever since Ray Bourque was a junior, he has been compared to Bobby Orr. In Boston, Orr is a legend. He played

10 years with the Bruins, from 1966 to 1977. With Orr, they won 2 Stanley Cups. Some people say he was the greatest hockey player ever. One thing is for certain: Orr changed the game.

Before Orr joined the Bruins, defensemen rarely scored. Orr was different. He brought offense to the defense. He was a smooth skater, an accurate passer, and a superb stickhandler. Just like Bourque is today. After Orr joined Boston, the NHL was never the same. It used to be rare for any team to average more than 3 goals a game. Defensemen rarely left their zones. Orr was a defenseman, but he played like a defenseman and a forward combined. In short, he was the first all-around defenseman in the game. For 2 years running, he won the scoring title. No other defenseman had ever done that before.

Soon, other defensemen tried to copy Orr's style. The game became more wide open. Teams started averaging 4 or 5 goals a game. Orr was the best of his time. And Bourque is probably the best of his.

Bourque himself says Orr was the best. Others usually agree, but not by much! Lemoyne said Bourque was the best defenseman ever to come out of the Quebec League— "a second Bobby Orr." Bourque's teammate, Terry O'Reilly, put it this way: "He has the same in-the-blood instincts that Bobby had. The way he turns and skates and makes plays, it's just like walking is for some people."

Park, like O'Reilly, played with both Orr and Bourque. He says Orr was the better skater. But Bourque is better in a crowd. When other players gang up on him, he can break free. "Ray is more of a magician," Park said. "He can do tricks with the puck." The Bruins' general manager, Harry Sinden, also was with the team when both played. He doesn't like to compare the two. He prefers to think of Bourque as a special player in his own right.

Maybe Sinden is right. Maybe when great players are

that great, it serves no purpose to compare them. Just watch them play—and enjoy!

Bruin Kingpin

One thing has always escaped Bourque and the Bruins: successful playoffs. In 1982–83, they came closest to it. Bourque was the top Bruin that year. Boston counted on him when they were in trouble. They never needed him more than in the series opener against the Nordiques.

The Bruins were in big trouble. Most of their top defensemen were injured. Only Bourque and Mike O'Connell could play. Their partners were rookies and minor-leaguers. It was up to those two. And they never played better. Boston hung on to win the first game, 4–3. But their big defensemen were tired. Heading into the second game, Bourque had an injury to his foot. He could have sat out, but that would have left the Bruins even shorter on defense. So he played for 40 minutes while hurt in Game 2. And he starred. Though injured, Bourque scored the tying goal. And O'Connell scored the winner. The Bruins won, 4–2. They were able to go on, and they won the series, 3–1.

Next, Boston won another playoff series, this time against the Buffalo Sabres. Finally, the team lost to the New York Islanders. But that was no shame. The Islanders went on to win their fourth straight Stanley Cup that year.

Bourque's fine play has continued through the years. The next season, 1983–84, he set personal highs of 31 goals and 96 points. And he has also starred for Canada's national team in 2 special series. Every few years, the best players in the world meet in the Canada Cup tournament. Bourque played for Canada in both 1984 and 1987. Both years, Canada won the Cup.

So, Bourque has a Norris Trophy and 2 Canada Cups. Only the Stanley Cup remains. With Bourque on Bruins defense, that dream may soon come true.

Ray Bourque won the Norris Trophy in 1987 for being the NHL's best defenseman.

The ref clears a path—quickly!—for a charging Goulet.

MICHEL GOULET
Quebec Nordiques

It could have been a miserable end to a miserable season. The Quebec Nordiques had come close to missing the 1986–87 NHL playoffs, but a late charge helped them to squeak in. Now, it was time to meet the Hartford Whalers in playoff round 1. The Whalers were a strong team. They had taken first place in the tough Adams Division. The Nordiques had finished fourth in the Adams.

On paper, it was a mismatch. And the first 2 games pointed to a Hartford sweep. Hartford won both. The Whalers only needed to win 2 more. Quebec had to win 4. But Hartford forgot about Michel Goulet. Goulet is the Nordiques' top left winger. When he gets hot, there is no better scorer in hockey. And against Hartford, he got hot.

The Whalers came to the Quebec Coliseum for Game 3. They were ready to push Quebec to the brink. But the Nords battled back. That night, Quebec toppled Hartford. Center Peter Stastny scored three goals. Goulet scored two. Quebec won, 5–1.

The next night, Goulet scored 3 goals and an assist in 1

game. Quebec took a 4-1 win. So the series went back to Hartford for Game 5. Now it was tied, 2 wins each. Both teams were halfway to victory. Hartford fans were getting worried. They were right to be worried, too. Goulet scored the winning goal as Quebec won again, 7-5.

The Nordiques were on a roll. Two nights later, they ended Hartford's season with a 5-4 victory. After the game, Goulet was very happy. His team had been the underdog. But they had taken 4 straight, and the victory was sweet. "Everyone in Hartford is thinking Stanley Cup," he said with a grin. "But first, they must come through Quebec."

Quebec then met Montreal in the Adams Division finals. The winner would meet the winner of the Philadelphia-New York Islanders series. And the winner of *that* series would go to the Stanley Cup finals. Quebec started strongly. The Nordiques won the first 2 games, but then Montreal won 3. Quebec battled back to tie the series at 3 wins each. But Montreal took the deciding game. Goulet bowed out a proud man. He and his teammates had taken Montreal—the defending Stanley Cup champion—to the limit.

It was a satisfying end to the season. Goulet had led all left wingers in goal-scoring. And again he was named to the NHL's first all-star team.

Secret Practices

How did Michel Goulet get to be such a great scorer? The answer lies in his boyhood days. Michel was one of 8 brothers born to the Goulet family. He lived on a farm near the small town of Peribonqua, Quebec. Peribonqua is about 150 miles north of Quebec City, home of the Nordiques. It gets cold there in the winters. That was fine by the Goulet boys! That meant there would be plenty of ice around. The boys would play all day on the pond near their home.

ABOUT MICHEL GOULET

Full Name Michel Alain Goulet
Birthdate April 21, 1960
Hometown Peribonqua, Quebec
Family Andree, wife
 Dominique, daughter (age 4)
 Vincent, son (age 2)
Boyhood Hero Bobby Hull
Outside Interests Managing private businesses;
 Mira Foundation (for the blind)
Hockey-playing Relatives Eric Goulet (brother)—
 Chicouhini, QMJHL

Young Michel learned to skate when he was 4 years old. With so much ice and so many boys, it was natural—they started playing hockey.

The boys didn't have a hockey teacher. They just put on their skates, picked up their sticks, and played. That kind of hockey is called "shinny." Shinny is fun, but it doesn't help a hockey player learn the game. Shinny players don't pass well. They usually don't skate well, either. But boy, can they shoot! And Michel was the best of them all in Peribonqua.

Michel could score easily. But he didn't really know the game of hockey. There was no organized league in Peribonqua. The town was too small. Children had to travel out of town to play with real teams. The nearest town with teams was called Mistassini. Michel started to play hockey very late. He didn't join a Mistassini team until he was 13. Many of the boys there had been playing for 5 or 6 years.

But he was willing to learn. He would show up for prac-

Opponents have to check Goulet closely to stop him from scoring.

tices. And he would play in the games. He had a good shot, and that helped. But his skating wasn't polished. He didn't know how to check. And his passing wasn't great. So, he vowed to improve.

Once, when he was 15, Michel figured out a plan. Someone lent him a key to the Mistassini town arena. He kind of forgot to give it back. Then he wondered: Would anyone miss this key? Maybe he could use it himself to get extra ice time. So, every morning at 5:00 or 6:00, he would visit the arena.

Swish! Swish! Swish! The only sounds were those of his skates gliding on the ice. He'd dig in with his blades and turn on the speed. He'd stop suddenly, sending ice chips flying. Then he'd start up again for another circle around the rink. He was making up for all the practice time he missed playing shinny.

The plan worked. Michel's skating improved. Suddenly, he was fast on ice! A good shot doesn't matter much if you can't get to the net to use it. Now, he had both skill *and* speed working for him. He soon became one of the best players in Mistassini midget hockey. What a dream it would be for a small boy from Peribonqua to make it in the NHL! But Michel had to face first things first in order for his dream to come true. And he must first play junior hockey.

One day, in the middle of the season, Michel was called by the Quebec Remparts—a junior team in the Quebec League. Would he like to play for them? He sure would!

Improving in Junior

So, in the 1976–77 season at the age of 16, Michel Goulet was one step from the pros. Now he had to work even harder. He had to be tough and play his best to keep up with the older players.

Goulet's coach worked with the boy to bring out his best.

> **ABOUT MICHEL GOULET**
>
> **NHL Team** Quebec Nordiques
> **Number** 16
> **Height** 6'1"
> **Shoots** Left
> **Best Asset** Slapshot
> **Position** Left Wing
> **Weight** 185 lbs.

The coach, Ron Racette, was patient. He helped him improve his skating. He taught him tricks about passing the puck. Even Goulet had much to learn about shooting at the junior level. The half-season was a success. In 37 games, he scored 35 points (goals plus assists).

Other teams were watching Goulet. The team in Laval wanted him. Laval offered to trade Mike Bossy for him. Bossy was a fine player in junior. He later became an NHL all-star with, of course, the New York Islanders. But the Remparts didn't go for the deal. They were happy with Goulet. He was young and had a great future ahead.

The Remparts were rewarded for sticking with Goulet. His training sessions with Racette helped. At the end of his first full junior season, he had 73 goals and 62 assists in just 72 games. That was good for any junior. For a 17-year-old, it was terrific. The performance won him a spot on the league all-star team.

The Remparts were very happy. Goulet would play for them another 3 years—or so they thought. They weren't prepared for the World Hockey Association. The WHA was a professional league that played in the 1970s. It was the second best league. The NHL was always number one. And the WHA was always trying to catch up. One day, the owners in the new league dreamed up a plan to help it get some new stars.

WHA owners knew the NHL didn't draft juniors until they were 20 years old. What if the WHA signed players aged 18? Maybe then they could get some young stars. So the owners decided to sign the best "underage" juniors they could find. One was Wayne Gretzky, now with the Edmonton Oilers. Another was Michel Goulet. He was signed by the WHA's Birmingham Bulls for the 1977-78 season.

Young Pro

Goulet's only year in Birmingham was successful. He had been playing organized hockey only 5 years and now here he was, a pro. He knew he had a lot to learn. But it didn't stop him from helping the team. He scored 28 goals and 30 assists for the Bulls. His 58 points were second-best on the team.

After the season, the WHA and NHL announced they were merging. But the Bulls would be left out. The team would be broken up.

The Quebec Nordiques wanted Michel Goulet more than any other WHA player. But they would have to wait for the draft to get him.

When draft day came, the Nordiques were nervous. Would some other team pick Goulet before they could? But the Nordiques got lucky that day. They were able to snap up Goulet with their first pick.

The team now had a cornerstone. From the start, Goulet starred with the Nordiques. In his first NHL year, he scored 22 goals. That isn't many for today's Goulet, but it was plenty for a NHL rookie.

The Nordiques' coach that first year was Jacques Demers. Demers has been one of hockey's best coaches for years. In 1986-87, he won the NHL's coach of the year award. He always seemed to know how to get the most out of his players. The Nordiques said they wanted to win or

> **MICHEL GOULET'S ACHIEVEMENTS**
>
> **Led League In**
> Goals by left winger: 1982–83, 1983–84, 1985–86, 1986–87
> Points by left winger: 1982–83, 1983–84, 1986–87
>
> **Important Awards**
> Twentieth over-all in 1979 Entry Draft (Quebec's 1st choice)
> NHL Second All-Star Team (1983)
> NHL First All-Star Team (1984, 1986, 1987)

lose with young players. Among others, that meant Goulet. He was nervous in the early going. He made mistakes. But the team stuck with him.

Coach Demers took some pressure off by saying he didn't expect the youngster to score goals. Goulet's job was to play defensively. He would check the other team's best players. And if he scored, that was a bonus. The move helped Goulet develop a good all-around game. He could always score. People knew that. Now, they found out that he could check, too.

Goulet kept on improving. The next year, 1980–81, he scored 32 goals. And the year after that, he scored 42. He was emerging as one of the NHL's best left wingers. He set himself a new goal. When Goulet entered the league, he wanted to score 25 goals in a year. Now, he wanted to score 50. A 50-goal year is something special. In the 1980s, only about 7 players a year have scored 50 goals. That's not very many, considering that each year about 500 players play in the NHL.

Michel Goulet: young star for the Quebec Nordiques

Fifty-goal Gunner

Goulet started quickly in the 1982–83 season. By midseason he was on pace for his first 50-goal year. He was being spoken of in the same breath as Bossy, Gretzky, and the Montreal Canadiens' great Guy Lafleur. That year, Goulet wound up with 57 goals. That was just 3 short of the all-time season record. Next year, he followed up with 56! Both years, he was named to the official all-star team. Goulet also established himself as a good passer in 1983–84. His passing led to 65 assists. Altogether, he scored 121 points—a new record for left wingers.

Entering 1984–85, Goulet had a chance to set another record. Three other left wingers had scored 50 goals or more 2 years in a row. None had ever done it 3 years running. His chances looked good. After 38 games, he had 31 goals. But then, in the first game of the new year, he broke his thumb. Just when the Nordiques needed their star left winger most, he missed 11 games.

He knew he was needed. He could have stayed out of action longer, but he decided to play with a cast on. How could the game's best left winger score with a cast on his hand? No one knew how, but he managed. He kept on scoring as if he wasn't injured at all. With 8 games left in the season, he hit the magic 50 mark yet again! The fans at the Coliseum went wild. They showed their favorite how they felt with a long, loud ovation.

He ended the year with 55 goals. Goulet and his Nordiques went all the way to the Campbell Conference finals—one step away from the Stanley Cup final series. That was farther than a Nordique team had ever gone before.

No left winger seems to play as well year after year. In 1985–86, Goulet again topped the 50-goal mark. And this time, it was in an important game against Montreal. Whichever team won this showdown would win first place in the Adams Division.

The Canadiens jumped out to an early 3-0 lead, but Goulet was determined to win. He assisted on 2 goals to cut the lead to 3-2. Then he scored his 49th goal of the year to tie it. Montreal went up, 4-3. But no lead is safe when Goulet's on the ice. He scored his 50th to tie it again. Then he added 2 more goals! The Nordiques sailed on to first place, winning 8-6.

When Michel Goulet skated onto the ice at the Nords' next home game, he heard wild cheering. The fans at the Coliseum were giving him a standing ovation. Their hero had led the team to a division title!

WAYNE GRETZKY

Last amateur club: Sault Ste. Marie Greyhounds (OHA).

Season	Club	League	Regular Season GP	G	A	TP	PIM	Playoffs GP	G	A	TP	PIM
1976-77	Peterborough	OHA	3	0	3	3	0	—	—	—	—	—
1977-78	S.S. Marie	OHA	64	70	112	182	14	13	6	20	26	0
1978-79	Indianapolis	WHA	8	3	3	6	0	—	—	—	—	—
1978-79	Edmonton	WHA	72	43	61	104	19	13	10	10	20	2
1979-80	Edmonton	NHL	79	51	86	137	21	3	2	1	3	0
1980-81	Edmonton	NHL	80	55	109	164	28	9	7	14	21	4
1981-82	Edmonton	NHL	80	92	120	212	26	5	5	7	12	6
1982-83	Edmonton	NHL	80	71	125	196	59	16	12	26	38	4
1983-84	Edmonton	NHL	74	87	118	205	39	19	13	22	35	12
1984-85	Edmonton	NHL	80	73	135	208	52	18	17	30	47	4
1985-86	Edmonton	NHL	80	52	163	215	46	10	8	11	19	2
1986-87	Edmonton	NHL	79	62	121	183	28	21	5	29	34	5
NHL Totals			632	543	977	1520	299	101	69	140	209	40
WHA Totals			80	46	64	110	19	13	10	10	20	2

WENDEL CLARK

Last amateur club: Saskatoon Blades (WHL).

			Regular Season					Playoffs				
Season	Club	League	GP	G	A	TP	PIM	GP	G	A	TP	PIM
1983-84	Saskatoon	WHL	72	23	45	68	225	—	—	—	—	—
1984-85	Saskatoon	WHL	64	32	55	87	253	3	3	3	6	7
1985-86	Toronto	NHL	66	34	11	45	227	10	5	1	6	47
1986-87	Toronto	NHL	80	37	23	60	271	13	6	5	11	38
	NHL Totals		146	71	34	105	498	23	11	6	17	85

RON HEXTALL

Last amateur club: Brandon Wheat Kings (WHL).

			Regular Season								Playoffs					
Season	Club	League	GP	W	L	T	Mins	GA	SO	Avg	GP	W	L	Mins	GA	SO	Avg
1981-82	Brandon	WHL	30	12	11	0	1398	133	0	5.71	3	0	2	103	16	0	9.32
1982-83	Brandon	WHL	44	13	30	0	2589	249	0	5.77	—	—	—	—	—	—	—
1983-84	Brandon	WHL	46	29	13	2	2670	190	0	4.27	10	5	5	592	37	0	3.75
1984-85	Hershey	AHL	11	4	6	0	555	34	0	3.68	—	—	—	—	—	—	—
	Kalamazoo	IHL	19	6	11	1	1103	80	0	4.35	—	—	—	—	—	—	—
1985-86	Hershey	AHL	53	30	19	2	3061	174	5	3.41	13	5	7	780	42	1	3.23
1986-87	Philadelphia	NHL	66	37	21	6	3799	190	1	3.00	26	15	11	1540	71	2	2.77
	NHL Totals		66	37	21	6	3799	190	1	3.00	26	15	11	1540	71	2	2.77

PAT LaFONTAINE

Last amateur club: 1984 United States Olympic Team.

Season	Club	League	GP	G	A	TP	PIM	GP	G	A	TP	PIM
				Regular Season					Playoffs			
1981–82	Detroit Compu.	Midget	79	175	149	324	12	—	—	—	—	—
1982–83	Verdun	QMJHL	70	104	130	234	10	15	11	24	35	4
1983–84	U.S. National	—	58	56	55	111	22	—	—	—	—	—
	U.S. Olympic	—	6	5	5	10	0	—	—	—	—	—
	NY Islanders	NHL	15	13	6	19	6	16	3	6	9	8
1984–85	NY Islanders	NHL	67	19	35	54	32	9	1	2	3	4
1985–86	NY Islanders	NHL	65	30	23	53	43	3	1	0	1	0
1986–87	NY Islanders	NHL	80	38	32	70	70	14	5	7	12	10
	NHL Totals		227	100	96	196	151	42	10	15	25	22

RAY BOURQUE

Last amateur club: Verdun Black Hawks (QMJHL).

			Regular Season					Playoffs				
Season	Club	League	GP	G	A	TP	PIM	GP	G	A	TP	PIM
1976-77	Sorel	QMJHL	69	12	36	48	61	—	—	—	—	—
1977-78	Verdun	QMJHL	72	22	57	79	90	4	2	1	3	0
1978-79	Verdun	QMJHL	63	22	71	93	44	11	3	16	19	18
1979-80	Boston	NHL	80	17	48	65	73	10	2	9	11	27
1980-81	Boston	NHL	67	27	29	56	96	3	0	1	1	2
1981-82	Boston	NHL	65	17	49	66	51	9	1	5	6	16
1982-83	Boston	NHL	65	22	51	73	20	17	8	15	23	10
1983-84	Boston	NHL	78	31	65	96	57	3	0	2	2	0
1984-85	Boston	NHL	73	20	66	86	53	5	0	3	3	4
1985-86	Boston	NHL	74	19	57	76	68	3	0	0	0	0
1986-87	Boston	NHL	78	23	72	95	36	4	1	2	3	0
NHL Totals			580	176	437	613	454	54	12	37	49	59

MICHEL GOULET

Last amateur club: Quebec Remparts (QMJHL).

Season	Club	League	GP	G	A	TP	PIM	GP	G	A	TP	PIM
			Regular Season					Playoffs				
1976-77	Quebec	QMJHL	37	17	18	35	9	14	3	8	11	19
1977-78	Quebec	QMJHL	72	73	62	135	109	1	0	1	1	0
1978-79	Birmingham	WHA	78	28	30	58	65	—	—	—	—	—
1979-80	Quebec	NHL	77	22	32	54	48	—	—	—	—	—
1980-81	Quebec	NHL	76	32	39	71	45	4	3	4	7	7
1981-82	Quebec	NHL	80	42	42	84	48	16	8	5	13	6
1982-83	Quebec	NHL	80	57	48	105	51	4	0	0	0	6
1983-84	Quebec	NHL	75	56	65	121	76	9	2	4	6	17
1984-85	Quebec	NHL	69	55	40	95	55	17	11	10	21	17
1985-86	Quebec	NHL	75	53	51	104	64	3	1	2	3	10
1986-87	Quebec	NHL	75	49	47	96	61	13	9	5	14	35
	NHL Totals		607	366	364	730	448	66	34	30	64	98
	WHA Totals		78	28	30	58	64	—	—	—	—	—

ABBREVIATIONS USED IN STAT SHEETS

Leagues
NHL	National Hockey League
AHL	American Hockey League
IHL	International Hockey League
WHA	World Hockey Association
OHN	Ontario Hockey League*
QMJHL	Quebec Major Junior Hockey League*
WHL	Western Hockey League*

*indicates Junior League

Scoring Details
GP	Games Played
G	Goals
A	Assists
TP	Total Points
PIM	Penalties in Minutes
W	Won
L	Lost
T	Tied
GA	Goals Against
SO	Shut Outs
Avg	Average (used interchangeably with GAA)
GAA	Goals Against Average
MINS	Minutes Played

About the Author

RICHARD BEALES' earliest childhood memories were of playing "road hockey" in his driveway with older boys in his neighborhood. As he got older, he discovered that his writing was better than his athletic ability. He pursued journalism in high school and university studies, covering school sports events.

When not busy at his job editing copy for *The Hockey News*, Richard enjoys watching pro hockey and baseball. Richard, his wife, Miriam, and baby daughter, Rachel, now live in Ajax, Ontario.

This is Richard's first book for children.